I0879744

Put Your Hand In Mine

Put Your Hand In Mine

Elaine Woo

Garry Thomas Morse, Editor

Signature Editions

Cover design by Doowah Design.
Photo of Elaine Woo by S.W.

This book was printed on Ancient Forest Friendly paper.
Printed and bound in Canada by Hignell Book Printing.

We acknowledge the support of The Canada Council for the Arts and the Manitoba Arts Council for our publishing program.

Library and Archives Canada Cataloguing in Publication

Title: Put your hand in mine / Elaine Woo.
Names: Woo, Elaine, author.
Description: Poems.
Identifiers: Canadiana 20190057769 | ISBN 9781773240473 (softcover)
Classification: LCC PS8645.O475 P88 2019 | DDC C811/.6—dc23

Signature Editions
P.O. Box 206, RPO Corydon, Winnipeg, Manitoba, R3M 3S7
www.signature-editions.com

To my dear family, near and far, and to my readers

CONTENTS

Embrace

Inside: an octopus writhing.
Microscopic viewing reveals
wavering bands, fabric palm fronds submerged.
Blunt-struck: Neither you nor I can seed hope
or straddle future as well as past
merely comb through history
enumerate the illumined advances
and grunge of errors.

Internal Peace

Shielded by mind-walls, I sweep away impinging affairs into blue-grey, wrestle with my own hungers, cross-eyed obligations

duties to the material, to the other and the other, to social geographies, to the vocation that sustains, provides non-monetary riches. As for the physical

diminished and more; the others, boundaries trenched without pitch, buck off power grip(e), ensuing peace; the societal, expanding lofty dimension, solid wisdom, and the calling, green growth.

Upon horizon's tableau, change begins with the inner field. The inner becomes the social, a web of difference stretching elastic. Peace begins with inner contemplation foments deliverance from undeserved torment.

Softly

fibrillation, nation, demi-god, school:

Mahatma Gandhi's ideals

non-violent civil disobedience

catalyzed sweeping change

knotted diverse threads into one

protested by thunder of the unarmed, marching

frayed, stumbled rope

teachings lost:

many hands and mouths minds frag and maim

Tossing & Turning

labyrinth, a mine: veins, coins, horns, leaves protrude from a sea of green, snag all who enter

canary song: a hung mist, notes dart through taffeta air, linger tremulous

carbon beads on tree digits

ram leap over cloud
  hit the corner 7-Eleven, thirsty for a Big Gulp
  shop carnage before returning to the hospital

short reptilian legs clump
  over mist-lip, crocodile jaws agape
  saw-teeth stained with carnal consumption
  yellow eyes ice, in pursuit

big horn distracts with beef bait
  knocks self off sky-locked transport
  sinks through multiple levels
  of heavenly mist, lands hoof-flat
  on grey murk
  prehistoric beast still visible
  gashing leg on jagged rock

guards self, uppermost priority
  big sheep retreat
  into subterranean mind
  left cheek moist
  head aches, tosses
  the scoundrel a steak

Spotlight

blue and orange
manacled to side mirror shadow
he rubs the scuff mark
on his handcrafted Italian shoes

I hold high a looking glass
image holds the glare of him

rotary-legs churn him to his square
he clambers up his statue's torso
pores exude perspiration and oregano scent
long hair a grapevine
drops from stone shoulders
kicking at litter at bronze base
laying dandelion bouquet at figure's feet

how to draw the tarnished
to the lip of his consciousness?

I ink on paper his fear of vanishing
poetic voicing; medicine

garbage-filled gutters
stench permeates
tired red brick buildings
caught in fade of clematis stars
he clenches shut his eyes
withers and slouches

Writhing

Through gargantuan speakers, scraping cochleae
woodlands aural-raped
python outside margins
imprisoned by synthesized explosions
metamorphosed energy under this threat
air ignited
ruptures into black smoke

Put on a Happy Face

He angles receptionist against round of water cooler:

his hairy face presses into hers *Use your integrity*

His lips spar: *never seen you smile*

some straddle Mt. McKinley

others never leave base camp

some are first to break the tape at the finish line

others limp in with a bad race time

She masks a smile, grinds her heel into his instep:

Sir, dictate script—I will

type it out.

Ooh, do tell me more.

Links artistic: on an island in the devastated sea

my betrayer, my soulmate, and I upbraided by society
with minutes to catch discharge-wings
to the capital city, a hub
of validation.
Forlorn on a rutted road near
a pride of biplanes, our feet beat
cruel pavement. I bear two faux-fur
packs, strapped across
shoulders, my freight
an exuberance of concepts.
One, vermilion
hope. The other
black and white motif; separate pouches
of fear and illumination.
We fly across a rivulet, land afloat midway
on optimism to beaming
the synapses of mind-parliament.
Signage gestures
at shimmering right brain. The traitor, a missile,
steams across indigo to the wharf
where ferry anchors to the bulwark payload.
My confidant and I race in a dinghy
through the channel towards shore, waves
vacuum at our skiff, splinter it on a shoal,
he broken the turncoat forsook
reached the banks of intuition first, mood
wavering, back-floats: an impulse buoys
him aloft.
Of a passing sea captain I implore
neurological passage to
acceptance through the murk.
Privately, the old salt decides
[No] vetoes himself claims overloaded.
Night-mind seeks lodging in a windswept cabin
to await salvation on the buffeted shores
of postmodernism, seeking opportunity to launch.

The Myth of Barbie

Way back down the line of time, I desired the Barbie doll all the girls on the block owned: the fashion doll with fairy tale credits from Easy Bake pilot light to licensed pilot, serving homemade roasts as a flight attendant.

She speaks egalitarian: *my friends include Hispanic Teresa and African American Christie.* Or does she? All her friends bear dubious Caucasian features. Did the product designers accentuate their own desire as the only flight path?

One-sixth scale, Barbie is a stunning 5 feet 9 inches, with 36-inch bust, 18-inch waist, 33-inch hip, decreed of insufficient body fat to menstruate. A 1963 vintage Barbie book entitled *How to Lose Weight* trumpted Don't Eat! Not recast for a wider waist until 1997. Teresa and Christie in tandem: *Does Barbie knit vulnerability? Or punish?*

Research published in 2005 theorized that girls reject their Barbie dolls, punish them by decapitation or microwaving: a rite of passage and disavowal of their past "Barbie Syndrome."

This cultural icon doesn't live in my wide waist or psyche.
Kudos to you
Mom: you wouldn't allow me one, spared me ritual beheading.

Nationhood

Five-storey-high flags undulate diagonal.

Turquoise, brown, and purple, intention

wheels traversing freeway; voice box

for a state proclaiming a *we* that fences

us from them

Why emblem so noisily?

Why emblem?

World Politics

From sliver tree branch, squirrelly scold, barometer tail swishes.
He, vigilant over his acorn cache.

Black and white Minou perches neat on deck railing. Fur gown, masquerades
as a lady. Her tail, time-bomb-metronome. She bides her time.

What if a new present were chiselled out, cat sheathed her claws, ceased salivating?

No, feline crouches, haunches, compressed gallows.

Styrofoam Dross

waves mumble

slide towards shore's consciousness

encumbrance   broken Styrofoam dross

at hem of your sand

a plane guzzles phlegm

rap music tangent pounds at the frame—

invade your sphere, threat or laissez-faire?

worn calendar of a man in red leans on his wheeled assistant

roll-shuffles into bird sanctuary envelope

frowns grey soot

Boundary Lane

Low barometric reading, in blur of blackness
blue recycling box morosely
slams against porch slats, acquires splinters.
Neurotic forces agitating? Intruder?
Mystified, dreaming with eyelids raised
I animate the front door light and porch with transformation
from brilliant to dark, back and forth.
Theatre of the psyche: another box strains with plastic bags ill-
conceived for consumption
lid knocked hysterical, shrieks, faints onto deck.
Ghostly chewing shreds the indigestible.
I wish the phantom dyspepsia.
Hands panicky, I intensify the light drama, alternate
between luminescence and black space.
Ringed tail, barrel-derriere, finally flees, abandons, I, encroacher.

Pecking Order

Strut, prance, preen,
flaunt college insignias.

Fowl down deep-fried lobster claws
red cabbage hatted with sugared pecans where
drooling crows sally trays of delicacies
from table of opportune to table of opportune.

Frye ankle boots
cuffed skinny jeans trills
Yeah, I worked for Gap
in the 70's when they had
art work all over the walls.
Daydream-y black-feathered hostess scours
her basement suite's concrete walls
papered with dollar-store eye candy.

Class Hysteria

Hermes Ascot accompanied by Mulberry Hand Bang
scowls blue-murder; his hairline, a retracting tide
that furtive extra inch, her lips pressed clams, sighting
that Hamburger Head parked
in the narrow laneway
leaving a sliver of not quite
two inches for 50s Ford convertible
meticulously maintained
replete with faded paint job
cool dents
to squeeze by.
Hamburger Head watches their faint-hearted passage
through the sleeve of vacant airspace,
wondering if they were sour
from forty years of smelling
each other's farts
or did they net his thoughts
or did they grow anemic anticipating
unfashionable razzing
the length
of their recent acquisition?

Alchemical Fire

despaired of rehabilitation
from you, my gangrene and boils affliction
unconscious already embedded with shards
shot from the abyss
chorus shredding my sphere
alchemical fire from plasma screens
dogs bare secrets, passersby pry

the way you 'splained it
woman's world is small
man's world is large
my jaw gnaws offence to particles
brow abstracts into ridges
you offer cerebral myrrh:
you manage to do it all
career and home
snowflake tyrants rap
against our panes
Christmas lights fantasize the entire street

ironed pleats of loneliness
swore I wouldn't be Hoovered
in again but my flooding eyes
betray me oxygen intake plunges
hear quick feet tip-tap down our stairs
still, will remain vigilant over
my reactive pulse and breath
appestat closed for business
silence balances on a tightrope
the green tea tepid

An Ill Wind

cabbage butterfly dragged downdraught

by winds' torrent   recent shootings

invisible hand inking

cumulus-cloud

brushstrokes dark

grief of dirty underbellies

beetle scuttles as gusts holler

horsetails inclined to the past

lupines unwillingly bend

leaves demoralized

funnelling inland empty

tree upended with branches' claws

swinging ground-wards, trend of the world

scrape knotted hearts

what would it take to loosen

these most crucial of organs?

Some birds bob amid deadly flotsam

volcano tremors

everyone: come, open your eyes

Tumult

Grey clouds squat, dulling conifers

biting wind curls hair around ears.

Push on, dead leaves crackle underfoot

crumple, fragments.

Ashen curtain sinks

Feet, too hulking to drag across deck

of wooden bridge

floor sags into a net.

Sinking

in pools of milk of magnesia.

SLOOGE! OOGE!

Falcons dive.

This, maybe a video game: crawl midway before eyelids droop

Every muscle, drained batteries throat dry of words

mind manipulates bodily joystick

barrel feet clump on, falter.

Ambulance siren scrapes past.

Ambiguity of voices

peaks,

fades....

Feeling the Way

bleeding colours

hazier than the real tableau

broken-thermostat-delusion

path art a braid

entwining of light and shade strands

dandelion helices—*I sing the body electric!*

water daemons flit through meaning

trustworthiness, a boulder

every boulder, the thermostat whines blue

willow limbs drape mood

a curse abstract this labyrinth

trip into gasps

skip stepping stones of robust bones

grin in hands

retain nylon plane, fly through tears in sky

Where Are All the Hens?

walking the edge of brine and clams

a storied place

from the pond of steel and glass radiating nasal duck chatter

mostly mallards

hens' allotted functions: domestic mess management

turmoil along a six-lane traffic

in monsoon season

shatter the towers

the road back longer than cross-Canada trek

leave the rain to its own devices

secure a final separation from that temporary acquaintance

roast needs defrosting

a lone hen flapping blazes berates three males

Share, Rogue?

Frayed over dog-yelping-mania
warriors protest my presence
hijack my fence-free yard
stake kingdom square by square.

Shall we sit round glass conference table
debate/negotiate this arm of terrain?

Celebrate the gavel: you get shrilling-rights-
of-expression, you, the victor.
A natural impulse—nonetheless—nerve-jangling.
My desire to bark back is impulse, too, scary escalation.
Am I fair to wish to curb this yip-yap, to desire you less vocal?
Likely, not.
You, domesticated creature, are supposed to be man's best friend.
Be my friend, too. Let me park my feet in this wooden teepee
doggedly embrace your canine angst.

Unfettered

all sense of time a mist, stitches
root under tread, presser foot unimpeded
French seams as thought, lanes marked
ripping life's road, synching limbs
eyes pinned, mind steeping reverie
garment's padding against lacerations
gauze, mother of pearl
                                        the gulf

Dwindle

eagles SOS on sky's ceiling

robins   wrens   finches

black-capped chickadees   blackbirds summit

blue maw lifts patch over eye, sighting erasure of a key cue

hail   rice grain needles tattoo

overflow ditches, bogs

over castling of perceived pawns

The Sky Is Seeping Black

swamp-ice-platters

grass tufts amber-brown   nature's winter ennui

chill sinks its incisors

puncturing eyelet in my neck

i wind my haunted arms

around my ribs

shrug tight my sweater funnel

a muffler-less car desecrates

the felt of night

driver and i—each equally tethered?

linger in the black swirling skein

Alternating Tones

entombed tree root in gravel path   mysteries of fate, misery, elation

embroidered bodies of trees

bird sonar

echoes sense   enormous detours

encouraging gains

scrutiny finds   1) wild roses   2) clouded-sun arrival

imposition of penalties   cause a tidal wave

umber of brambles   red salmonberries   invisible birds, their song ripe in scrub tangle

cones loosened from evergreen branches

waves sweep sand hem, bring in, bring out

paints a vast passage   surf climaxes, crashes

spent

vinyl spins

Vein Affect

We were fuzzy-precise. Not quite disconnected.
Her, sandals-clad, torso draped, in my foyer, hypnotized by empty frames
her uninvited parents, toddlers bulge through doorway
a crew vying for bathroom-relief, shooting
ammonia vapour out the door they forgot to close
leeches latching on for gratis dinner.
She: *You need lots of company.*

Our gap: San Andreas Fault. With song information entered, can browse for a song.

I crave solitude: introvert, you know. Cul-de-sac: laburnum and alders unshaven, off-leash-dogs harassing cats. Should ignore her quote from her guru, *A powerful mind has enemies, a peaceful mind has friends.* Strange, heard her cleaver her partner with mathematics, stone her kids into beaconing friends through darkening woods.

By default, I shriek apart the air.

Bleached paper white, sweat pearls her forehead, ache radiating her shoulders-wide, chest, too. ANGINA cries. Extended family fans her, strokes forehead beneath her hyena brow. 911. School bawls, graffiti scars obscure windows. Fire trucks, police, ambulance wail in, sea of red. Pulse normal, blood pressure low, respiration rate healthy, temperature normal, vegan-norm. EKG, blood tests recommended. Ambulance livid, derailed by her Munchausen syndrome. My exhaustion splinters rewind button, rallies white noise self-defence.

To download music and other audio files, I shut door on Brutus. Fate of ogres: hell's basement retreat. Summon a thumbnail and then an index nail of acceptance. Might I add all my fingernails? Manually manage playlist.

Hilltop Town, Italy

With each hairpin turn we bend
up incline to a village edged in
stone walls' parchment tones.

Save for muffled exchange of a knot
of young men in threadbare poly sweats
hands working cigarettes
devastation of flip-flops, shuffling feet
playground hushed.

We choke down bitter espressos
tip generously but are smothered
by a retiree's nicotine clouds.

Picking at a Scab on My Wrist

My shadow paces, footsteps parse time
    as I recall your shattered hip

A nervous storm, a wake of papers
    synapses, spark plugs

Swells of energy
    traversing continents to you
    my violin weeps

Sensory-absent when I was twelve
    from your kidney surgery

Metal strikes metal, with industry.
    Geese burn eastwards
    I, absent from their flock,
    wish to be centred in their letter V

Picking at a wrist scab
    red startles up
    I tattoo my brain cells—
    stopwatch, alarm clock:
    visit to passport office
    synchronize
    the day before Christmas Eve

Riverside

Red triangles twist
behind a veil of brittle leaves
brushed by water feathers.
My eyes tilt on the river's surface
water a blurred lens, articulate
voluptuous egg-ripe salmon bellies.

Oscillate through.

Strand

shades of betray, mutter the gods

howling rains pelt Olympian mountain aerie

rap funicular on its ascent

zip up to chalet

more pedalling cyclists than ever scaling octaves

circle to river arm

a ferry garbles a water ruffle

H & M, Benetton play light chemical notes

warm draughts volley a *hurrah* at fewer diamond mines

dipped sales of bloodstones

din revives life

bystanders in polyester fleece

permanence of fibres chills

they gaze at the tender flesh of their palms

whisper *what can one hand can do*?

Greed

Grains spill from plated jaws.
The hog scarfs
every grain of corn in trough
stomachs a tempest upon finishing.
On stodgy legs, he waddles into barn
plotting for a hostile takeover of the feed pails
rouses Farmer Brown who clouts
the swine on his snout. Undeterred
he thrives on the cancer of power
rips away, squealing for more.

Truth Bombs

Droning, ego pinnacles
in pride
plummets into valleys of rage
swaggers through groves
of glass trees
stretches on void jags
light bomb explodes
escalator to fullness

Material Concern

distressed denim, frayed holes, knee tears

patchwork, colour-block skirts

raggedy handkerchief hems

gypsy-hobo looks, dreadlocks, scuffed boots

cigarette butt–strewn sidewalks

she sports decay: counter culture? labourer empathetic?

impoverished affect?

fashion coup d'etat?

price tag, telltale?

tagging?

No Visibility Problem

Aegean turquoise brown-stained carpet:
once the hue of the sea.
Dew claw marks hardwood floors.
Wash basin, clamshell. Window
curve bending water.
Iron-leafed banister rounds up-down
hewn-slate steps.
Walk-in closet: full of Aphrodite.
Hangs her mate's three outfits near
the exit. Brags she gardens
in sateen.

Misalignment

Lugubrious walls, front desk candles,
reception staff, beauties, robed in black.
iPads mounted, affixed to white seats.
In flounces through the door, poly lace, a face
body melon-pale, ironed
gaunt bones unmasking chemical dalliance
anything to wrench back the minute hand.
Botox for her *chien* next?
I'm there for eczema salve
not to paralyze
character creases.

Imagine. She plunks down
dough for bread, sandwiches for the hard up
rather than winkle out those wrinkles
Suddenly, she and her bones are lovely.

Earth Song

in the howling

wilderness

Gauguin-yellow sun laughs

wisps of hollow reed notes, vines entwine the air

tufts of green whiskers root sand peaks

a coot nods on grey-green whorls

distant serrated pinnacles

a soft presence

draws her sketchbook from her bag

pencils mountain, sea, earth

a blue heron fishes

as raindrops blur light

she shuts her pages

Father and Daughter

You shared where to wind
a pinky 'round one end
wrapping yours over the other
encouraging me to make a silent wish.
We each yanked, the break yields
me the longer part of the wishbone.
Lyre notes bejewel the air.
Knew it wasn't magic, you didn't pull as hard as
you could have.

Healer, with that split, we are linked always.

Shooter

The tide subsides
reveals a fair-haired urchin
thorns embedded in his face
a gun poised—his hand
lips rat-a-tat at me
I catch his bullets in my palms
melt them into lead for poems

No Safe Moves

mudslide sweeps homes down hillside

mother closets my toddler-self in early death
i lodge baby finger
between open door and jamb crevice
yearning to brake
                                        fate
she blots out my red jumper
infant lungs, finger, rupture
                                        no safe moves
purple infuses through
flesh   bones   fractures deep

Uncomfortable

Eight-year-old me, naked in porcelain tub.

Mother truncates my bangs

abbreviates the sides into commas

crowns herself the fairest one of all.

Diorama: Headache

deep in vampire hours

on stage beneath her eyelids

phone rings manically with reminders of dinner
from lampooning teacher, trickles through backdrop
of dark prairie, a former artist steals props

broken concrete slab balances
askew   atop the peak
of her scalp   held aloft by turtle-leg stumps
     aggregate grinding
she teeters forward, slipping a step
tumbling   *nuit blanche*

Unsought Advice

loops a hairy appendage
in the front window,
another, scrapes paint off the sill,
jams adipose and bulbous head through,
paw punches the air and lectures:
That couch your cat used as a scratching
post, exercising her compulsions, has to go.
Pleather emotions much more desirable.
A red coat of paint on the walls will lend
an elegant vibration. Rid yourself
of your photo memories. Looks
like a shrine. Your seashell collection,
a scattered mess. Clump your concepts together.
Mind your look of space.

Peel durian.
Assemble redolent diced fruit salad.

Mother and Daughter

In peacetime in the new world
she commandeered the dishes
into precisely lined-up towers
in the sink, stalked crumbs
on the linoleum, detonated
over her daughter's refusal
to rinse off

Her daughter marshals
stained bowls and plates through soapy water
voices hailstones over her head

Cold and Hot

snow dust lights her face

awakens in her a prickling-heated anxiety

too engrossed in forest-bathing and meditation

late picking up her kids from school

starlings contentious

chill overwhelms her struggle against time

washed up on gravel banks
an acned orange block
refusing the wisdom
that surely comes of accumulated algae growth

she notes the sight with her camera

hot blood surges through her veins quickens her pace
she rushes to her jeep

means to make amends to her children

her tires spin on ice   her forehead slumps over steering wheel

she hopes to be rescued

Escape Route

Upon meeting, she and I split into distant oppositional points, water skeeters bumping and separating, as she snarls: *There is more to life than looking good.*

Should I cloud my face, erase the genetically given, abstract my fingernails into cerebral claws, dumb myself to match her unsaid take on my appearance?

If heated further, will I rub the corners of my temples, believing, *I shall not spoon-feed myself her insecurity.* Or will I fume, *Gonna avoid her until hell scorches the tarmac of the earth!!!*

Placing a doorstop on my thoughts, I wonder, *Maybe it was my fault wearing a floral dress and conjuring her?*

She pushes and shoves her lasagna this way and that. *I can't eat!* hysterics. *Man, my head.* I have no trouble eating my salmon salad. Inside, my thought bubbles grow arms and fingers, gather *chi* close to myself, and breathe in, exhale her. She hails a server to box up her food, feels sorry for her chronic troubles and regrets travelling downtown to meet me. In spite of it being my treat.

Shrinkage

New spackle not even set. Boxes laddered
atop one another, unpacked.
Fire the element beneath frying pan
antennae, peppercorn eyes
triangular bodies erratically jag across
white enamel stovetop followed
by tidal throng.

Spatula misses target for lack of hand-eye alignment.

Beeline   for the bathroom for Raid
lips contort   brows accordion pleat.

Lift my weighty comforter soaking
in the bathtub, a swarm of rust-brown cockroaches roil forth
from their clandestine sanctum.

Invasion of uncertainty   adrenals foreground, arteries dilate
shrinks judgment.

Venal?

lament up the incline imbroglio
mosquitoes orgy-gorge on me
hover, buzz, sting, draw blood en masse
I bat at them, vexed
palms become fly swatters
my desire to escape pain fires molten
careen down slope's backbone

feet pelt architecture
of linen earth

vermilion beads my face, torso

delve in portals to curiosity
wonder about their story

For Akiko

The year you turned seventy, I emailed you.

Reply: *I had head surgery.*

Your emails and phone calls ceased. Though my writing robe bears tears

still, I knit scarves of other texts yarn of your memory.

Transition

First Nations skim through cool blue waters
inky dusk leaked from your paint brush
an earth-toned portrait of me, too, that resembled
someone else. Puzzled to be linked with soil
I nonetheless placed
the tan rendering in my salon.

You inhaled painting, stereotypes, too
that I didn't realize until I dismantled my own thoughts decades later
open sometimes, you in red shorts, a mauve halter top to weed
your artistry blossoming nasturtium gardens, your faded scarf.
For hooking up your stereo, you gifted bountifully
one of your prints—my first real art.
Years slid by, palette of my memories, erased colours.
I missed our artistic bond
my idealized image of you, I phoned. A murmur
breast cancer.
Dropped by the old neighbourhood,
rang your bell, peered through your glass-panelled back door, seeing
things unfamiliar, grey shadows of furniture...dissolution.

now is not a unity

I wade in hip high   you cry a reservoir of tears for

you   arborite courtesy   offering seats   obsequious reflections

good on you   stinky worn hiking boots gift

altruism's self-back-pat [there's something self-serving to helping out]   offer false ears

chainsaw my conversation sheared thoughts

white chocolate chips appeasement

blemished shirt offering   red offence at refusal

friendly chat with my dog   shirk

from touching *Winston*   big teeth: fence gates hold me at time-ransom

oh have to take the laundry in

wrong outfit nothing co-ordinates brushing teeth

what's wrong with posing as a plane for my dad, my spread arms as wings?

i'm one hour late? laminate smile

fighting words   *don't open the windows   it's baking today*

sitting in my wide-open

backyard, *You'll leave your house*

to me, won't you? I would take such

good care of it   I lock my tongue   my hands grip

empty pan

Rope

stuck in a well

water surface ripple-fraught

chains of skimming ovals,

rotate: blocks   alphabet of depression

daylight of idealism snuffed

crawling on my hands knees slipping

skidding along murky bottom until

a crack in the stonework

seeps   in an idea:

rope up or down

live this present

not that

not then

or that apex   future,

with each now   this

plunge

        progress

Salon Hierarchy

with metal-precision,
his hands thread
in   out of my tresses,

   the frame: packed with spices
   wisps of accented English
   conversation, hairdressers break
   for Tupperware-packed lunches
   bucket lists of lifeguard prospects,

he enquires about Christmas
and New Year's

   his time off a strand of two days
   worked Boxing Day, New Year's Eve.

a bulky blonde in red
diagonals across mirror's length,
downpour of voices fills
the chairs vacant a moment before

   directional lines: the staircase: in the chairs sit
   the fortunate with the wealth of leisure time
   while working women and men stand,
   wield scissors and razors

a geometric repeating pattern.
how likely to be broken?
not to matter who occupies the chair—
should financial recompense recognize
those with the tools are not less than
not placeholders who bow and snip

Stop the Winds

Our unexplained
house, mortal electric body: lantern reverse-lit
a whirr, power silenced, an absence
open my third eye

Contemplate the batter swirl of black and grey
I'm cellophane-mouthed
swollen skies eruct all their wrath
cedars entangle   dishevelled bracelets

Winds vie for attention, excise
tree limbs — by involuntary surgery
sting our roof, vulnerable trunks sway
lose momentum

Psychosis of storms past
heighten the scream of this one
allow me a mannequin of calamity
swirling about an axis of lack of choice
I chisel chip by chip through ice   reclaim quiet power

Night Dimension

Furnace: backbone cracks.

Bulbs cast the only light

in the house. Radio voices rebound

off ceiling, threads weave a vocal cocoon.

Wheezy snores

hinges, floorboards rest.

Pantry moths breathe their last

in the glue of spider traps.

Spiders paint Kevlar

on our window sills.

Silk luminous under the moon.

Empty & Full

You kick when you see me

I turn to the duality
of blank space

My shadow tills the garden

last house at the bottom
cherry blossom–lined
nasturtium, geranium slope
street of my childhood.
As we converse, growth hormones
of his dreams seep out:
entry to writing school. Suspicious,
I circle his house three times.
He wants me badly and insists on it
hiding with my parents, Creativity and Muse,
at their home in a sumptuous tropical outpost.
Shadow slides under my nails,
pulses along my blue veins,
sinks into my pores.

At the island retreat, I pluck greenbacks
from my satchel for a sanctuary hiatus.
Mother Muse orders pork-shrimp wonton
from room service.

Prophesies a shaman,
sipping potency
{*soul food overly rich*
conceptual staple grains adequate}.

Dark glows my eyelids
sheens my terrestrial mind
willows my procrastination
staminas late nights of artistry.

Then, a door.

Great Company

Galumphed mewling
verbal-pitchfork-prodded
string unwinding down Alpen trail
in Edam sunlight
amidst sharp peaks
doused our hair and faces
with water bottles
we looked like drowned cougars
attempting to cool
not adapting to sticky tees, clammy feet, aching legs

We see in mountain meadows
the way standing zazen cows graze
the creatures *simply are*
their bells faint
tails brushing

Debt

Spider pauses on her silk nexus considering the wet that pelts her abdomen. Eight legs consider   an aluminum ledge.

Mottled mushroom, an awning for ants and other modest behemoths of the forest.

Iridescent mussels on slick rocks by the jagged shore, whether or not the tide should bring them plankton, they rooted cling.

Indebted to those of soil, oceans, the blue.

Bald Eagle

Creekside in my hazel tree. Mathematically statuesque.

Algorithm of white chest, brown wings, head white, beak yellow.

Coming Home

For Anna

Your hospitality extended: fizzing elderflower juice
from green genie bottles. Downing the bubbly drink
my taste buds smile in pleasure.

Behind us, your diffident tabby cat tiptoes from room to room, unfazed by my
presence in her country. Her acceptance comes by way of slinking round my legs.

Your embroidered boho tunic speaks artistry and home.
Calendar time marks the long highway between our visits, yet little has changed:
being with you is an easy chair.

Without ache in your voice, you speak of your loss of vision in one eye. You have full
spectrum light adaptation, computer screen adjustment. Maybe this is an opening, not a
closure.

We speak the parlance of book cover art, paper tones, typescript, ways to hook
an audience, learning French via poetic engrossment. Your kudos swing my world.

Our words slowly trickle low.

Wild Nature

Ivy-spade faces tenaciously inch up fir tree

persistent, leafy vultures

thrive until I pluck

their lifelines, green prints still evident

however cultivated, wild nature prevails

Bereft

Down a pebbly
road, we skid, weave

round and round, a ribbon wound

in diagonals along

an inverted cone, rocks

anxiety spasms constellation-ward.

Together in a Fred Flintstone heap

little stones embed.

We thread base-ward. Our car splits

fragments jet asunder

synapses flow lava

burnt hope
ashen tracks
you in your ethereal vehicle

I, in a clay one

You soar into lilac ether.

I skid into brown loam
whipped.

Seconds Rest

Crow lay, shielded by hostas,

Featherless patches, white down silence.

Moments sieve by, seconds rest.

Comrades flock on the grass

code-cacophony honours the fallen.

Black mass: yowling

visible hand unified in bereavement.

Isn't that something?

Mystical in moonlight cast, silhouetted

tense against pockmarked concrete

black pits spotlighted in cold white

owl torso in profile, beak, tri-tonal

cat's cradle of branches, sprawl of crow's feet

freed from shadow by wings

we have but legs for flight

cut out for certain levels of dark

Stoking the Siren

drench of a night   sightless-darkness

radio interview over in most-pained part of town
rush back to car

after unlocking, driver's side door swings wide open, wedges on the curb

pulling while seated inside, no go

fears of violence and deranged worry intestines

trying to free door from the sidewalk
heavy hands thud on shoulders   a vise
bind-weed around neck
whip-spins me
rattles, me a maraca
mind: a prison door   bolts him in isolation
with vermin starved for entrails
throat: a siren hobbled
Can we help? emerges feminine from the corner
serenely he drops chokehold
soft-foots across the street   seamless with the black sky

wheeze, *no   I'll see a doctor tomorrow*
collapse in car-safety
careen homeward   erect a Great Wall

try to castrate memory of him   wall is crumbly, hole-ridden

Police comment: *he just had a bad day*

Man! Freebies!

Shadows of highrises lean imperiously

over

youthful whiter-than-white pearl-toothed

women and men who pitch

Free pop! Free!

from behind a silver-steel food cart

Passing hands nab the gleaming cans

A homeless man, withered, compressed face

pokes in, takes the chemical-promise liquid

steps over to a nearby rubbish bin,

peels back the pull tab   sloshes orange carbonation

onto pavement, meticulously flattens empty can

retains the true value of aluminum

Casually, he returns for another, angles

bin-side again, empties, flattens, stores

returns for another, returns

returns

Mechanical In-equilibrium

force exerted

old sign painter beyond breaking

silence   he plunges

evicts the air

sun: a red ball

ashes rain

Suit of Lights Flickers

Matador feet, unbridled dance
faces square the gored one.
Dust clouds plume.
He waves aloft red fists
shakes out quivers.

Cold sweat pearls.
Wipes brow, cheeks
smears grime down cratered face.

Brown sacrifice dips head low
obsidian eyes trickle injury.

Cynic

brood clouds

    false starts

bitter chocolate stalagmites

loll in the cavern of mouth

read this as self and other poison

labour to remedy   unconscious roots torn

—a home more natural

Over the Fence

Old codger Darren blames his anus
boils on his neighbour Merry Mae.
Oozing gangrene
these fetid annoyances entrench
him in constipation.

He staggers about

accuses, blithely judges
hemorrhoids throb.

Snarls, *Move!* to Merry Mae.

She breaks into song. Her gospel-organ voice
chords dry laundry on his clothesline.

He unpegs her laundry
smile crooked.

Her voice peaks, drops
fallen laundry forgotten.

Canada Day

Returns desk biz.

Cashier: black suit wears her, as does red lipstick and big hair.

Uncertain from this vivid image before me, I extract

black jeans from my bag.

Hi, these don't fit.

She, barricaded lake, requests receipt and credit card

impeccably glides through charge reversal.

Queueing behind me, virtually invisible in grey, two elderly women.

As I leave the scene

one gushes to the clerk

I've never seen anyone wear

lip colour as well as you.

Dam gates retract; a warm cascade issues

from behind the counter

wishes them, *Happy First!*

wishing I could buy into that.

Template

Unwound a spool of time   hung it up to cure
amid blush/white roses enquiring of light
patterned waffles of almond-brown soil
sable-tipped palm tree fronds
big sigh of escaping cars
diminished sun

feet whine, eyelids flicker
waylaid by calluses of malaise
desire to clasp something/anything
with the aim of appeasement

mind ravenous *mmmrrhh*

lay imaginary footprints on pavement
set toes in front of each other, step, step off

later, wonder why that didn't come to mind before

Gazing at My Internal Warts

We have met the enemy and he is us.

—*Pogo* by Walt Kelly

Gouge at them, dig-heave, dig-ho
See-here, see-there

Exit through fire escape
open window, gaping door

Leave me atriums, bay windows
balmy weather

Reflexively cringe
breathe them and breathe them

Pit away, craving.

Falling Leaves

woman leavens, loosens harness

bold bones stark, released from shackles of beauty, folds

autumnal face, winter-silver hairs

she will wear red unexampled

flicker firm, navel ablaze

perspective, distant horizon approaches

loss, a lightning bolt grounded

Compartments

A nautilus shell, chambers
walled from the others

This is how, intake of fresh nutrients over cascade of self
and time feasible. From room to room
sieving yesterday from the silt of today
straining now from the white sands of tomorrow
still grains catch in the crevices
some lodge grating
some fall away

Fractured

Pebbles gouged in my knees, stamped pits in my palms
crept, upslope a gravelled shaft
mannequin of my old woman self on my youth borne
through hernia telescoped the tunnel
sea cobalt, cold, glimmering
radiant, streaked with plastic scraps

I signalled the elderly one
cement bags upon my back
her rheumy eyelids
crack a slit, survey impending bends
I tremble mightily that I might see
I tremble, hands, feet frigid

Until Just a Paste-Spit Remains

stripped appendages vie high   enclose their secret: a yearning for raw
earth   meringue of cloud cover   chain of loved ones   hilltops barber-
poled in frost stripes   beanies for the crests   upper reaches a hive of
pressing thumbs   striations of the starved on (E-)bay's skin   rabid
currents scour away Facebook selfies
scam artists clad in Revenue Canada balaclavas   inbox oozes spam
garbourate   until just paste-spit remains
red canoe   freshly painted
lies   hull up   at trail's foot   turning the woods inside out

Arm's Reach Away

Not exempt from the rent of loneliness
torn by barbed wire of misunderstanding.

Creek ripples register a companionable *shrr shrr*
fronds sweep the air in reply
camellia platters, red buds of depth
wild rhododendrons trumpet
planetary dispatch—lively communion

leaches through this isolate cloak.

Acknowledgments

A huge thank you to Karen Haughian for bringing me into the Signature Editions family and to Garry Thomas Morse for his brilliant edits. This book is really a collaboration with many (and you know who you are) I discussed the poems with. I owe all a great thank you. Without you this book wouldn't have been possible.

Thanks to the editors, versions of these poems appeared in:

"Styrofoam Dross" and "Dwindle," *Ricepaper Magazine.*

"Spotlight," *Your One Phone Call*, Wales.

"Truth Bombs," *Uut Poetry*, USA.

"Alchemical Fire," *Your One Phone Call*, Wales.

"Shooter," *Bone Orchard Poetry*, UK.

"Riverside," "Great Company," "Debt," and "Bald Eagle," *Royal City Poets: Anthology*.

"For Akiko," *Loose Leaf*, Toronto.

"Tossing and Turning" and "Pecking Order," *The Literary Commune*, Stafford, England.

"Links artistic," and "Strand," *h&* (handandpoetry.com).

"Nationhood" and "World Politics," Vol.44.3, *Grain Magazine.*

"The Myth of Barbie" and "Where Are All the Hens?" CWILA's *S/tick.*

"Falling Leaves," NationalPoetryMonth.ca2017: Angel House Press.

"Venal?," "My Shadow Tills," "No Safe Moves," "Shrinkage," "now is not a unity," "Salon Hierarchy," "Bald Eagle," "Tumult," and "Until Just a Paste-Spit Remains," *Experiment-O:* Angel House Press.

"Picking at a Scab on My Wrist," *Prism International.*

"Template," "Gazing at My Internal Warts," "Seconds Rest," "Cynic," and "Mechanical In-equilibrium," *The Elephants.*

About the Author

Born in Saskatchewan, moving to the West Coast as a young child, Elaine Woo is a poet, librettist, comics creator, artist, non-fiction writer, and video-maker. She studied creative writing and psychology at the University of British Columbia. Her work has been published in Canada, the US, the UK, France, and Hong Kong, and appears in print or online in *Prism International*, *Grain*, *The Maynard*, *The Elephants*, *Arc Poetry*, *carte blanche*, *West Coast Line*, *Otoliths*, and *h&* and in the anthologies *Sustenance, Veils, Halos & Shackles: International Poetry on the Oppression and Empowerment of Women*, *Shy* (winner of an Independent Book Publishers silver medal in 2014), *The Enpipe Line*, and *V6A*. An alumna of the Vancouver International Song Institute's (VISI) Art Song Lab, her art song collaboration with composer Daniel Marshall won a Boston Metro Opera festival prize in 2013. Elaine's first full-length poetry collection was *Cycling with the Dragon*, published by Nightwood Editions in 2014.

Eco-Audit

Printing this book using Rolland Opaque 30 instead of virgin fibres paper saved the following resources:

Solid Waste	Water	Air Emissions
148kg	8,074 L	286kg